PRAYING
with Smith
Wigglesworth

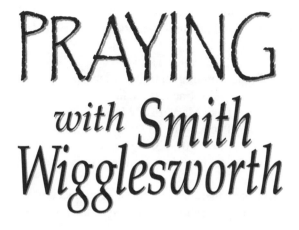

PRAYING
with Smith
Wigglesworth

Larry Keefauver

CREATION
HOUSE
Orlando, FL

Creation House
Strang Communications Company
600 Rinehart Road
Lake Mary, FL 32746
Phone: 407-333-3132
Fax: 407-333-7100
Web site: http://www.strang.com

All Scripture quotations are from the King James Version
of the Bible.

This book is dedicated to Judi, Amy, Peter and Pat; the Keefauvers, Laings and YMCS partners who prayed for me.

Contents

Preface

or Smith Wigglesworth, praying was an act of faith. Over and over again he would declare that faith must act. One of the most important and essential actions of faith is prayer.

Born in 1859 in Menston, Yorkshire, England, Smith Wigglesworth was converted at age eight and dramatically touched by God forty years later. Wigglesworth was thrust by God into a worldwide, evangelistic ministry helping lay the foundation for today's Pentecostal and holiness movement. He worked for years as a plumber and helped his wife, Polly, with a small mission in Bradford until his death at age eighty-seven. The prayers in this volume are inspired by Smith in the context of his messages and sermons preached through Britain, Europe, the States, Australia and New Zealand.

Each prayer is rooted in Wigglesworth's original words. At times Wigglesworth's preaching and praying seemed to flow into one stream of thought and inspiration. His words were both proclamation and intercession, spoken at God's throne and overheard by the listening ears of men. As a result the power of God was manifested in mighty miracles and healings accompanied by astounding deliverances and even the raising of the dead.

Wigglesworth believed that when the Holy Ghost fell on him or anyone else, that person was in the very presence of God and able to minister His power, presence and miracles of the Spirit. Wigglesworth took seriously Jesus' declaration that His disciples would do mightier acts than He did (John 14:12). So Smith Wigglesworth acted and prayed in faith trusting God to respond immediately with signs and wonders.

The purpose of this volume of prayers is to move the believer from faith to action. When we pray, heaven and earth are moved by the power of His Spirit. Take hold. Be inspired. Unlike theologians and scholars who intend their words to evoke study and reflection, Wigglesworth desired that his words would motivate his hearers to faith, prayer and action. Praying with Wigglesworth is a call to action to touch the heart of God and to shake the culture in which we live with Holy Ghost power.

Introduction

 ow can this volume of prayers best be used? Here are some possibilities:

- Read one thought from Smith Wigglesworth, the Scripture and the prayer aloud each day. There are enough prayers for three months of daily praying.
- Read through a quote, Scripture and prayer together with a spouse or prayer partner.
- Memorize the quote, text and prayer. Meditate and pray them through daily.
- Form a prayer group. Use the prayers as a time to launch your group into corporate prayer.

- Use the Scripture or the topical indices to determine which prayer best fits your need for prayer each day.
- Listen to the Holy Spirit. Ask Him to guide you in selecting the prayer for each day.
- Remember, the purpose of these prayers is not that they be read, but that they be the springboard for praying.

Lord Jesus,
I give You praise for the privilege of praying
through these thoughts of Smith Wigglesworth
with Thy Word inspired by the Holy Spirit.
Use this volume for Thy glory.
Cover each reader with Thy blood and the Word
of Thy testimony. In Jesus' mighty name, amen.

The Praying
Wigglesworth

he power and fruit of Smith Wigglesworth's prayer life was demonstrated in the awesome meetings he held in which thousands were saved and healed. Wigglesworth talked little about his private praying with one notable exception — praying in tongues. In fact, as he preached and taught, tongues would often burst through his messages and immediately interpretation would follow. Praying in tongues was as natural as breathing for Smith. He often spoke of the experience in South Wales at Sunderland, which transformed his life, initiated his ministry and became the bedrock of his powerful evangelistic meetings.

The Welsh Revival had swept through South Wales

under the leadership of Evan Roberts in 1904. By Roberts' side was Alexander Boddy, the vicar of All Saints' Church in Sunderland. He and his small parish prayed earnestly for two years that revival with an outpouring of the Holy Spirit would break out at their congregation. Boddy invited a Norwegian methodist pastor, T. B. Barrett, to stop by and preach in his pulpit on his way to America. While in New York City the year before, Barrett had met with some new Pentecostals and experienced praying in tongues. He reported, "I was filled with light and such power that I began to shout as loud as I could in a foreign language."[1] Returning to Europe and sharing his experience, Barrett gave impetus to the Pentecostal movement on the continent.

So in Sunderland Barrett shared his prayer experience on a Sunday evening in September 1907. Praying in tongues visited that small gathering starting a revival that would change Wigglesworth's life on Sunday morning, October 26. Prior to this time Smith had helped his wife, Polly, with meetings at their tiny Bowland Street Mission. However, he never spoke and left the preaching to his wife.

Believing there to be more spiritually for him to experience, Smith traveled to Sunderland and found himself in the parish hall of All Saints' Church. That providential

Sunday morning, Smith recounts, "Three times in that prayer meeting I was smitten to the floor by the mighty power of God." He spoke of a fire burning within him and by Tuesday morning, "the fire fell and burned in me until the Holy Spirit revealed absolute purity before God..." Still, he had not received his prayer language. For four days he sought God and then asked Mrs. Boddy, the vicar's wife, to lay hands on him. As she prayed the power of the Holy Spirit seized Smith and he cried out, "Clean! Clean! Clean!" He began to pray in tongues and glorify his Savior. "I could no longer speak in English. Then I knew that though I had previously received anointings, now I had received the baptism in the Holy Spirit as they did on the day of Pentecost."[2]

Smith then asked Alexander Boddy if he might speak to the congregation. Wigglesworth's first sermon so stirred the congregation that fifty of those present were filled with the Holy Spirit and spoke in tongues.

As Wigglesworth's ministry expanded to include preaching throughout Europe, the States and Australia, he continued to emphasize praying in tongues and the baptism of the Holy Spirit. His prayer life was filled with praying in the Spirit. His close associate, Albert Hibbert, related:

In his prayer life, he often prayed in the Spirit. He

did this because he said things which are too deep for our minds to grasp and too profound for our language to utter. These can only be appropriated by our spirits.

Since Wigglesworth was a man with no education, his grammar was very poor. However, when he interpreted his own utterance [in tongues], he spoke English grammar of the highest standard. Without a doubt, this occurrence was miraculous. Through learning the secret of praying in the Spirit, Wigglesworth touched realms far beyond himself.

One could often see a change in Wigglesworth as he prayed. He would continue speaking in an unknown tongue as he moved into another realm. He often prayed this way when faced with a desperate need...The Christian church needs to learn the secret that Smith Wigglesworth learned and walked in: this secret of praying in the Spirit.

Wigglesworth's life changed when he prayed. Preaching at Glad Tidings Tabernacle in 1922, he spoke of the change that praying brings into our lives.

"I know this as clearly as anything, that no man can change God. You cannot change Him. There is a word in Finney's lectures which is very good. 'Can

a man who is full of sin and all kinds of ruin in his life change God when he comes out to pray?' No, it is impossible. But as a man labors in prayer, and groans, and travails because his tremendous sin is weighing him down, he becomes broken in the presence of God. When properly melted in the perfect harmony with the divine plan of God, then God can work in that clay where before He could not work. Prayer changes hearts but it never changes God."[4]

In the depths of prayer, Smith Wigglesworth entered the heavenly realms and communed with his beloved Lord. He was transformed and changed. May you be so changed and transformed as you pray.

---

1.   Jack Hywel-Davies, *The Life of Smith Wigglesworth* (Ann Arbor, Mich.: Servant Publications, 1987), 63.

2.   Ibid., 67-69.

3.   Albert Hibbert, *Smith Wigglesworth The Secret of His Power* (Tulsa, Okla.: Harrison House, 1982), 62-64.

4.   Smith Wigglesworth, "Faith (Part Two)," message presented at Glad Tidings Tabernacle, 3 August 1922, 2.

In the Words of Wigglesworth...

"Holy Ghost people have a ministry."

Gifts of Healing, p. 1

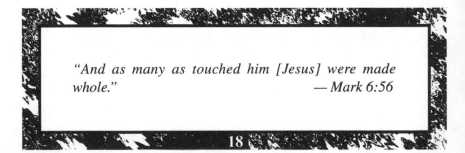

"And as many as touched him [Jesus] were made whole." — Mark 6:56

Dare to Believe
for Every Healing

Holy Ghost, so fill me
that I might bring forth healing power.

Purge any fear from within me as I pray for the sick.

I believe that You, Holy Ghost, have filled me
with the power to dare to believe for every healing
through Your healing gift.

Amen.

In the Words of Wigglesworth...

"The gift of the Holy Ghost, when He has breathed in you, will make you alive so that it is wonderful."

Gifts of Healing, p. 3

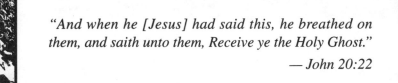

"And when he [Jesus] had said this, he breathed on them, and saith unto them, Receive ye the Holy Ghost."

— John 20:22

Holy Ghost, Breathe on Me

Holy Ghost, breathe on me.

Quicken me.

Pour the Father's jealousy over me.

Fulfill Your purpose in me.

Grant me a glimpse of the grandeur of Thy glory.

Amen.

In the Words of Wigglesworth...

"If you dare ask for any gift, really believing it is a necessity gift, if you dare ask and will not move from it but begin to act in it, you will find the gift is there."

Gifts of Healing, p. 3

"And all things, whatsoever ye shall ask in prayer, believing, ye shall receive." — *Matthew 21:22*

Dare to Ask and Act

Almighty God,

I will not be moved,

Nor will I cease from asking,

Until I receive all

That You purpose for me.

Amen.

In the Words of Wigglesworth...

"Claim your right. Claim your position. You never get a gift if you ask for it twice. But God will have mercy upon you if you stop asking and believe."

Gifts of Healing, p. 4

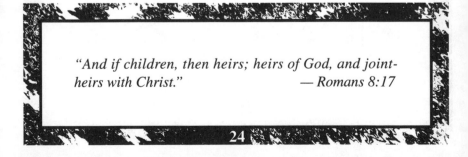

"And if children, then heirs; heirs of God, and joint-heirs with Christ." — Romans 8:17

Claim Your Right

Lord, I come not as a beggar but as an heir.

Verily, a joint-heir in Christ.

In His power and authority, I claim my right.

Standing in the position of grace,

Knowing that just one request is enough,

I now ask for Your gift.

Believing Your Word, I now receive.

Amen.

In the Words of Wigglesworth...

"The gift of healing is a fact. It is a production. It is a faith. It is an unwavering trust. It is a confidence. It is a reliability."

Gifts of Healing, p. 6

"And Jesus, moved with compassion, put forth his hand, and touched him, and saith unto him, I will; be thou clean." — Mark 1:41

The Gift of Healing

I pray for the gift of healing,
    not for self,
        not seeking signs,
            not for glory,
                not to marvel,
                    not to wonder.

I pray for the gift of healing,
    for others,
        for the sick,
            for the afflicted,
                for the hurting,
                    for the wounded,
                        for the pained,
                          for the broken.

    I know, Jesus, You will grant my request.
    For such touches Your heart. Amen.

In the Words of Wigglesworth...

"Let us repent of everything that is hindering us. Let us give place to God. Let us have no self-righteousness, but let us have brokenness, humbleness, submittedness."

Gifts of Healing, p. 7

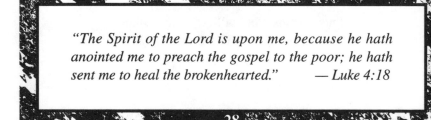

"The Spirit of the Lord is upon me, because he hath anointed me to preach the gospel to the poor; he hath sent me to heal the brokenhearted." — Luke 4:18

Losing Self in Him

Lord, break my heart with Your love.
I repent of being unloving.

Lord, break my heart with Your righteousness.
I repent of self-righteousness.

Lord, break my heart with Your humility.
I repent of my pride.

Lord, break my heart with Your submission.
I repent of my rebellion.

Thus broken, then mend my heart,
O Thou Healer of the brokenhearted.

Amen.

In the Words of Wigglesworth...

"May we be dead indeed and alive indeed with refreshings of the presence of the most high God."

Gifts of Healing, p. 7

"And you hath he quickened, who were dead in trespasses and sin." — *Ephesians 2:1*

May We Be Dead Indeed!

Jesus, teach me to die to self,
to be crucified with You;

That I may know the fellowship of Your sufferings,
and the power of Your resurrection.

My mortal body merely exists without
the breath of Your Spirit.

My thoughts merely wander without
the renewing of Your Spirit.

My feelings merely expend without
the refreshing of Your Spirit.

My spirit merely rambles without
the quickening of Your Spirit.

Spirit of God, quicken the whole of my being.

Amen.

In the Words of Wigglesworth...

"The baptism of the Holy Spirit is a smashing of the whole man and a compassion for the world."

Unconditional Surrender, p. 1

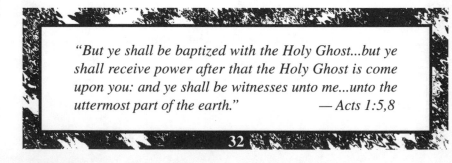

"But ye shall be baptized with the Holy Ghost...but ye shall receive power after that the Holy Ghost is come upon you: and ye shall be witnesses unto me...unto the uttermost part of the earth."　　　　— Acts 1:5,8

God, Smash Me!

God, smash me,
That I might be baptized in the Holy Spirit.

God, smash me,
That I might have compassion for the world.

Amen.

In the Words of Wigglesworth...

"What shall we do to receive it [the baptism of the Holy Spirit]? Repent! Repent! Repent!"

Unconditional Surrender, p. 1

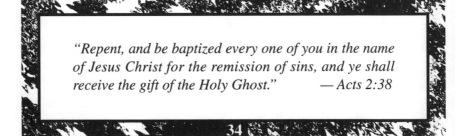

"Repent, and be baptized every one of you in the name of Jesus Christ for the remission of sins, and ye shall receive the gift of the Holy Ghost." — Acts 2:38

Receive the Baptism of the Holy Spirit

Jesus, I repent.

Forgive me.

Jesus, I repent.

Save me.

Jesus, I repent.

Cleanse me.

Jesus, I repent,

Baptize me with the Holy Spirit.

Jesus, I receive.

Amen.

In the Words of Wigglesworth...

"Turn your back on every sense of unbelief, and believe God."

Faith, p. 10

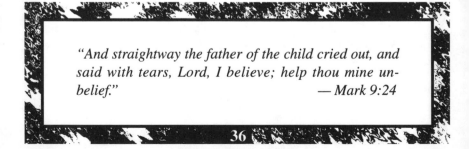

"And straightway the father of the child cried out, and said with tears, Lord, I believe; help thou mine unbelief." — Mark 9:24

Turn Your Back on Unbelief

Lord, I believe.

Help Thou my unbelief.

Lord, I trust.

Dispel my mistrust.

Lord, I have faith.

Overcome my lack of faith.

Lord, I believe You.

Amen.

In the Words of Wigglesworth...

"God wants us to be holy. He wants us filled with a power that keeps us holy."

Filled With God, p. 1

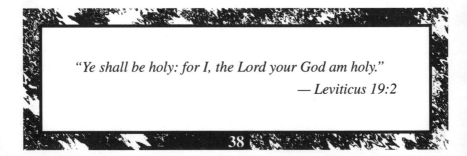

"Ye shall be holy: for I, the Lord your God am holy."
— *Leviticus 19:2*

Be Holy

Thou art holy, O God.
Thy holiness burns as an all-consuming fire. Consume me with Thy fire. I desire to be holy even as Thou art holy. Set me apart from the world that its bondages will have no tie on me. Fix my heart solely on things above and not on things below. Create within me a hunger and thirsting after Thy purity and holiness.

Thou art holy, O God.
There is none like Thee. No one else can touch me, fill me, baptize me, anoint me, use me, empower me and love me like Thee. There is none like Thee. All others that pretend holiness are not. All gods who vie for Thy place are in no place. All idols who pretend to be like Thee are not. Create in me a yearning for all Thou art and for nothing Thou art not. Consume me with holy fire. Fill me with desire solely for Thee.

Thou art holy, O God.
Thou alone can make me holy. I implore Thee. Do it now! Amen.

In the Words of Wigglesworth...

"To be filled with God means that you are free: full of joy, peace, blessing enduement, strength of character, formed fresh in God and transformed by His mighty power so you live, yet not you, but another lives in you."

Filled With God, p. 2

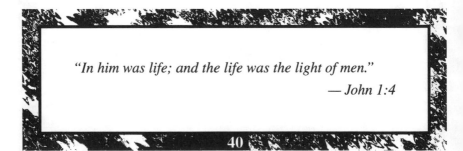

"In him was life; and the life was the light of men."

— John 1:4

Filled With God

Father, fill me with Thyself,

That I might know Thee.

I yearn passionately for Thy life,

Joy,

Light,

Peace,

Blessing,

Enduement,

Strength of character,

Fresh, transforming power.

How I desire to live, not just exist.

Amen.

In the Words of Wigglesworth...

"We must move on to let God increase in us for the deliverance of multitudes, and we must travail through until souls are born and quickened into new relationship with heaven."

Floodtide, p. 1

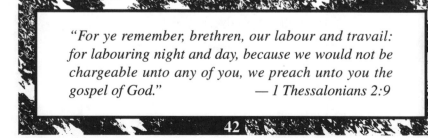

"For ye remember, brethren, our labour and travail: for labouring night and day, because we would not be chargeable unto any of you, we preach unto you the gospel of God." — *1 Thessalonians 2:9*

Travail for the Lost

O blessed Savior,

I bow before Your throne,

Beseeching You to send the Holy Spirit

That He might convict and save the lost.

Convict and save lost family and friends,

Lost church members,

Lost coworkers,

Lost government leaders,

Lost world leaders,

Lost religious and irreligious peoples.

For all the lost, I travail before Thee
with tears and moanings. Amen.

In the Words of Wigglesworth...

"The Lord is the great promoter of divine possibility, pressing you into the attitude of daring to believe all the Word says. We are to be living words, epistles of Christ, know and read of all men...We are living in the inheritance of faith because of the grace of God, saved for eternity by the operation of the Spirit bringing forth unto God."

Floodtide, p. 2

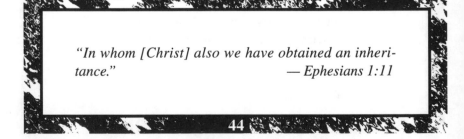

"In whom [Christ] also we have obtained an inheritance." — *Ephesians 1:11*

44

Living in the Inheritance of Faith

Lord, press me into the attitude of daring
to believe all the Word says.

Lord, make of me a living word, Your epistle,
to be read by all.

Lord, grant me a vision of my inheritance in You,

That I might lay claim to both Your present and future,

So bringing heaven to earth that You will quicken all
things into beauty,

Manifesting Your power through me to the world —

That power to lay hold of omnipotence
and impart to others the Word of life.

Amen.

In the Words of Wigglesworth...

"If you are without condemnation, you are in a place where you can pray through, where you have a revelation of Christ; if you follow the definite leadings of the Spirit of Christ, He brings you to a place where you cannot have any fellowship with the world."

The Incarnation of Man, p. 1

"There is therefore now no condemnation to them which are in Christ Jesus, who walk not after the flesh, but after the Spirit." — Romans 8:1

Praying Through

Unveil my eyes, O God,
that I may discern the world from the divine,
that I may see beyond the visible to the invisible,
that I may have a revelation vision of Christ, my Lord.

Liberate my spirit, O God,
that I may follow the leadings of Thy Spirit,
that I may thirst for fellowship with Thee above all others,
that I may scorn the works of the flesh
while savoring the fruit of the Spirit.

Teach me, O God,
instead of praying about, to pray through the problem,
instead of praying for, to pray in the Spirit,
instead of praying to, to pray with Thee.

For it is my longing, O God,
to pray through my condemnation to Thy acceptance,
to pray through my prayer to Thy prayer,
to pray through my desire to Thy will,
to pray through my flesh to Thy Spirit. Amen.

In the Words of Wigglesworth...

"The law of the Spirit of life in Christ Jesus will make you free from the law of sin. Sin will have no dominion over you. You will have no desire to sin, and it will be as true of you as it was of Jesus when He said, 'Satan cometh, but findeth nothing in me' (John 14:30)."

The Incarnation of Man, p. 2

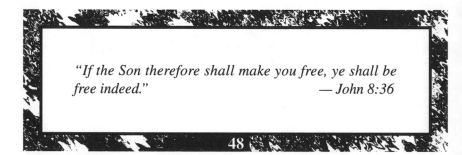

"If the Son therefore shall make you free, ye shall be free indeed." — *John 8:36*

Breaking Sin's Dominion

Free, O God, I'm free.

Free from the dominion of sin and death;

Free from the lies I tell myself
and the lies the enemy tells me;

Free from the desires of the flesh;

Free from the lust of the eyes;

Free from the pride of life;

Free from the law of sin;

Free from Satan's accusations.

Jesus, Thy truth has set me free. Hallelujah! Amen.

In the Words of Wigglesworth...

"The devil brings back to the minds of people those things which they did so long ago, and there they are, thinking about them day and night! There are two things certain:...that you never forget them...[and] that God has forgotten them. And the question is whether we are going to believe God, or the devil, or ourselves?"

Ordination, p. 1

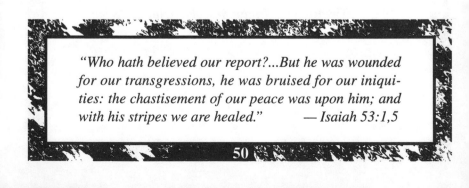

"Who hath believed our report?...But he was wounded for our transgressions, he was bruised for our iniquities: the chastisement of our peace was upon him; and with his stripes we are healed." — Isaiah 53:1,5

50

Whom Will You Believe?

Taking the thoughts of accusations captive,

I come to You, Lord Jesus, with this request:

That You would empower me to resist Satan
that he would flee,

And that You would remind me of my sin —

Not for the sake of condemnation, but for praise,

Praise that You died for me;

Praise that You shed Your blood for me;

Praise that You redeemed my life from the pit;

Praise that You have forgiven me;

Praise that You saved me from the wages of sin
for the wonder of heaven.

I choose to believe Your report and no other —
I'm forgiven! Amen.

In the Words of Wigglesworth...

"Now the Holy Ghost will take the Word, making it powerful in you until every evil thing that presents itself against the obedience and fullness of Christ would absolutely wither away."

Possession of the Rest, pp. 4-5

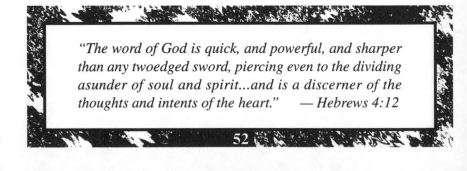

"The word of God is quick, and powerful, and sharper than any twoedged sword, piercing even to the dividing asunder of soul and spirit...and is a discerner of the thoughts and intents of the heart." — Hebrews 4:12

Prayer and the Word

Word of God, pierce me through with Thy sword.

Divide my soul and spirit, my joints and marrow.

Discern my thoughts and heart's intents.

Word of God, heal me throughout.

Heal my soul and spirit, my joints and marrow.

Heal my thoughts and heart.

I pray that Thy Word may rest so mightily on me,

That all sickness flees and all affliction breaks
under the name of Jesus.

Thy Word alone brings true and abiding rest. Amen.

In the Words of Wigglesworth...

"It is possible to be in the Spirit at the washtub, in the Spirit scrubbing floors, in the Spirit under all circumstances."

Possession of the Rest, p. 7

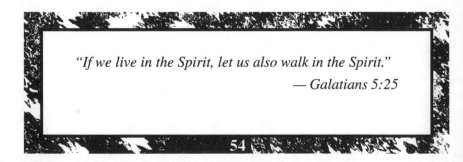

"If we live in the Spirit, let us also walk in the Spirit."
— Galatians 5:25

In the Spirit

In every task,

At every place,

Through every trial,

Within every blessing,

Under every situation,

Upon every departure or entrance,

Around every relationship,

Over every moment,

Let me, heavenly Father, be in the Holy Spirit. Amen.

In the Words of Wigglesworth...

"Oh, if you won't resist the Holy Ghost, the power of God will melt you down. The Holy Ghost will so take charge of you that you will be filled to the uttermost with overflowing of His grace."

Possession of the Rest, p. 8

"Be filled with the Spirit." — *Ephesians 5:18*

Filled to the Uttermost

Melt my resistance, Spirit Fire, that all dross might be consumed;

that all wood, hay and stubble might become ashes;

that all pride might be smashed;

that all hardness might be softened;

that all conceit might be broken;

that all bitterness might be rooted out.

Fill to the uttermost, Spirit Anointing, this earthen vessel of my being;

that I might overflow with grace;

that I might pour forth with living water;

that I might exude joy;

that I might pray without ceasing;

that I might live life abundantly. Amen.

In the Words of Wigglesworth...

"From his place in the wilderness, he [John] moved the whole land. God through him cried the cry of the Spirit. Oh, that awful cry. All the land was moved by that piercing cry. Some are ashamed to cry. There is a loudness in a cry. God is with a person with only a cry."

The Cry of the Spirit, p. 1

"The voice of him that crieth in the wilderness, Prepare ye the way of the Lord, make straight in the desert a highway for our God." — Isaiah 40:3

The Cry of the Spirit

Within and out of me, cry forth, Holy Spirit.

Cry repentance.

Cry forgiveness.

Cry hope.

Cry a new song.

Cry a heavenly language.

Cry for joy.

Cry good news.

Cry forth from within me, Holy Spirit.

Amen.

In the Words of Wigglesworth...

"But in these last days God will pour out upon all flesh the Latter Rain, and I believe all flesh will feel the effects of it...I believe that God would have us see that the Latter Rain has begun to fall."

A teaching on John 7:37-39, p. 1

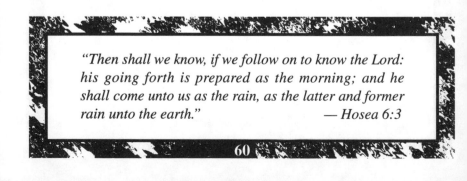

"Then shall we know, if we follow on to know the Lord: his going forth is prepared as the morning; and he shall come unto us as the rain, as the latter and former rain unto the earth." — Hosea 6:3

Latter Rain

Holy Spirit, rain on me.

Former rain fell on me at rebirth.

Now let Thy Latter Rain fall.

Drenched by living water, I seek Thy flood,

Not a drizzle,

Not a shower,

Not a passing storm,

Rather, pour out the flood of Thy Latter Rain
on the church;

That we might experience Pentecost anew. Amen.

In the Words of Wigglesworth...

"While I know that prayer is wonderful, and not only changes things but changes you...yet I tell you...that faith is the greatest inheritance of all."

Faith, p. 1

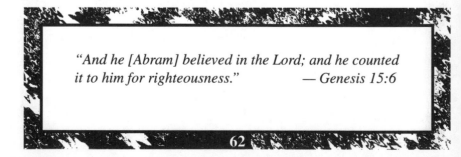

"And he [Abram] believed in the Lord; and he counted it to him for righteousness." — *Genesis 15:6*

Claiming My Inheritance

May God give me faith that will bring His glorious inheritance of faith into my heart;

> For it is true that the just shall live by faith.

May the Lord reveal to me the fullness of the truth that He gave to Abraham.

> Credit to me righteousness by faith, O God,
> Even as You did with Abraham,
> That I might receive the inheritance of faith,
> So as to be blessed and become a blessing to others.

My faith rests in nothing less than Jesus' blood and righteousness. Amen.

In the Words of Wigglesworth...

*"It is impossible, if God covers you with His righteousness,
for anything to happen to you, contrary to the mind of God."*

Faith, p. 3

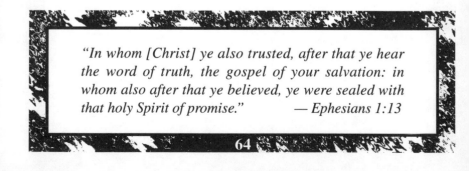

*"In whom [Christ] ye also trusted, after that ye hear
the word of truth, the gospel of your salvation: in
whom also after that ye believed, ye were sealed with
that holy Spirit of promise."* — *Ephesians 1:13*

Under His Covering

God, set Your seal upon me;
> That I may be covered by the blood of Christ and
> sealed by the Holy Ghost.

Cover me with Your righteousness;
> That I may believe every prayer I utter will bring
> Your answer.

Grant me Your righteousness;
> That I may see You and obey You in everything;
>> That I may know Your heart;
>>> That I may have my inner self revealed by
>>> Your Spirit.

I pray that You will set Your seal upon me;
> That the devil dare not ever break in where I am.
>>>>> Amen.

In the Words of Wigglesworth...

"I want you to see that you can be healed if you will hear the Word. Now there are some people who need healing; maybe some want salvation; maybe others want sanctification and the baptism of the Spirit. The Word says it is by faith, that it might be by grace."

Faith, p. 6

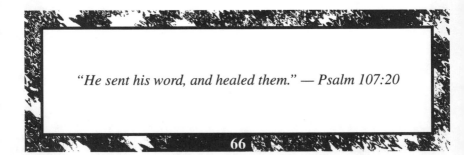

"He sent his word, and healed them." — Psalm 107:20

Healed by His Word

Jesus, by Your Word, I am saved and healed!

By Your stripes, I am saved and healed!

By Your wounds, I am saved and healed!

By Your blood, I am saved and healed!

By Your grace, I am saved and healed!

By Your touch, I am saved and healed!

Jesus, all that I am,

All that I will become,

All that I desire to be

Is by Your Word. Amen.

In the Words of Wigglesworth...

"One thing I know is that Satan does not know my thoughts; he only knows what I let out of my mouth."

Faith, p. 8

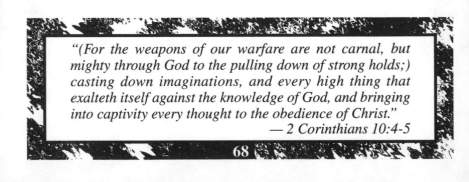

"(For the weapons of our warfare are not carnal, but mighty through God to the pulling down of strong holds;) casting down imaginations, and every high thing that exalteth itself against the knowledge of God, and bringing into captivity every thought to the obedience of Christ."
— *2 Corinthians 10:4-5*

Defeating Satan

In Jesus' name, I have victory over Satan.
> He cannot touch me or my family.
> He has no knowledge of my thoughts or my heart.

I crush Satan under my heel.

I command every thought to be taken captive;
> Every vain imagination to be cast down;
> Every high thing in my life that exalts itself to be made low.

Lord, grant me Your power to guard my heart and my tongue that I might keep my counsel ever before You. Amen.

In the Words of Wigglesworth...

"Can we be filled with a river? How is it possible for a river to flow out of us? A river of water is always an emblem of the Word of God — the water of life — and so when the Holy Ghost comes, He clothes and anoints the Christ which is already within the believer."

A teaching on John 7:37-39, p. 3

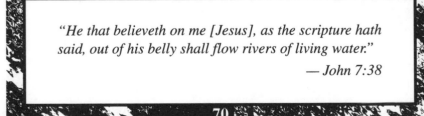

"He that believeth on me [Jesus], as the scripture hath said, out of his belly shall flow rivers of living water."

— John 7:38

A Flowing River

Flow, Spirit, flow,

Into me,

Through me,

Within me,

From me,

Out of me.

River of Life, flow;

Spirit of God, flow!

Amen.

In the Words of Wigglesworth...

"And do you not know that one little bit of faith which can only come through the Word of God is worth more than all your cryings, all your rolling on the floor, all your screaming and everything."

A teaching on John 7:37-39, p. 6

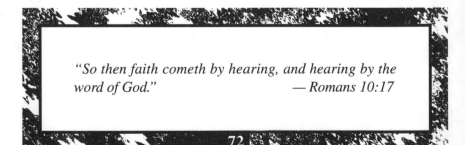

"So then faith cometh by hearing, and hearing by the word of God." — *Romans 10:17*

The Word and Faith

Jesus, sow into my life the seed of Your Word.
> Prepare the soil of my heart that I might not be
> hardened toward You:
> Pull out every thorny care of this world.
> Pulverize the rocky walls that come between me and You.
> Purge secret sins from my life.
> Purify my heart, so desperately wicked that at times I
> truly do not know myself.

Jesus, sow Your seed of faith into my heart,
> So that every mountain needing moving may be moved,
> And every mountain needing climbing might be scaled,
> And every valley passed through might be filled with
> the presence of Your Word.
> Hide Your Word in my heart so that every act and
> attitude that issues forth from my life might glorify
> You and build faith in others.

Amen.

In the Words of Wigglesworth...

"O, to live a holy life! What a zeal! What a passion! O, to live in all the beauties of all the glory and grandeur of the Holy Ghost! O, the fascination of the Christ of God makes me realize there is nothing in this world worth grasping."

The Abiding Spirit, p. 3

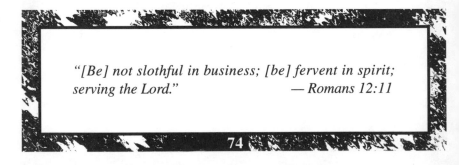

"[Be] not slothful in business; [be] fervent in spirit; serving the Lord." — Romans 12:11

Zeal for Christ

Christ,
Be Thou my fascination
that things of this world pale next to Thee.

Be Thou my zeal
that my enthusiasm for all else wanes.

Be Thou my passion
that I might be ablaze with holy fire.

Be Thou my glory and grandeur
that Thy image may be reflected in me.

Christ,
Be Thou my consuming love, my all in all.

Amen.

In the Words of Wigglesworth...

"If you see Him, you needy ones, you sinners, as you gaze at Him you will be changed. As you look at Him you will find that your natural body will change; a strength will come to you. There is life right through the focus that you get on the Son of God: a perfect transformation right there in His look."

The Abiding Spirit, p. 5

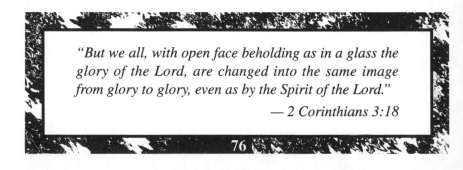

"But we all, with open face beholding as in a glass the glory of the Lord, are changed into the same image from glory to glory, even as by the Spirit of the Lord."

— 2 Corinthians 3:18

See Jesus

How I long to see You, Lord.
How my eyes need to focus on nothing but You.
How my gaze feasts upon Your loveliness.
How I need changing.

Transform me from dust to divinity;

from mortality to immortality;

from natural to supernatural;

from flesh to Spirit;

from weakness to strength;

from glory to glory. Amen.

In the Words of Wigglesworth...

"You cannot keep yourself. No man is capable of standing against the wiles of the devil by himself, but when you get Jesus in you, you are equal to a million devils. Are you willing to so surrender yourself to God that Satan shall have no dominion over you?"

The Abiding Spirit, p. 8

"Put on the whole armour of God, that ye may be able to stand against the wiles of the devil."

— *Ephesians 6:11*

Stand Not Alone

With You, Holy Spirit, I stand not alone.
>Arm me with God's whole armor.

Search me, Holy Spirit, unmask any portion of me that is
unsurrendered.
>Expose my hidden sin.
>Uncover my darkest secrets.
>Reveal my cesspools of unspoken lusts and desires.

Without Your unveiling of my hidden sin,
>I face unrelenting attacks of the enemy.
>Still, I know that there is no condemnation for those
>>in Christ Jesus.
>Take that, Satan. Yes, I'm guilty. No, you can't touch
>>me for I'm confessing all sin.
>I'm forgiven by Jesus;
>>I'm cleansed by His blood;
>>>I'm freed from every curse;
>>>>I am loved forever!

I declare that the only one defeated in my life is Satan.
Through Jesus' victory, I've won eternity. Hallelujah!
Amen.

In the Words of Wigglesworth...

"Fear is the opposite of faith. There is no fear in love, and those whose hearts are filled with divine faith and love have no question in their hearts as to being caught up when Jesus comes. The world is filled with fear, torment, remorse, brokenness, but faith and love are sure to overcome."

Believe! The Way to Overcome, p. 1

"For God hath not given us the spirit of fear; but of power, and of love, and of a sound mind."

— 2 Timothy 1:7

No Fear!

In You, Lord, I have no fear.

Quiet my anxieties about tomorrow.

Still my tremblings of inadequacy.

Remove my doubts.

Grant me serenity that flows from faith.

Fill me with power to replace my weakness.

Love me beyond my capacity to love myself.

Soothe my mind with Your tranquillity.

In You, Lord, I have no fear.

Amen.

In the Words of Wigglesworth...

"There is no limit to the power God will cause to come upon those who cry to Him in faith; for God is rich to all who will call upon Him."

Believe! The Way to Overcome, p. 2

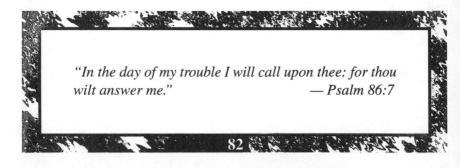

"In the day of my trouble I will call upon thee: for thou wilt answer me." — *Psalm 86:7*

In the Midst of Trouble

Almighty God, I'm troubled,

Attacked on every side,

Helpless to help myself.

I cry out to You for deliverance.

In Your power crush my enemies;

Subdue my critics;

Flood my drought with the wellspring
of Your living water.

In my day of trouble, deliver me
for Your name's sake. Amen.

In the Words of Wigglesworth...

"As your prayer rests upon the simple principle of faith, nothing shall be impossible to you."

Believe! The Way to Overcome, p. 2

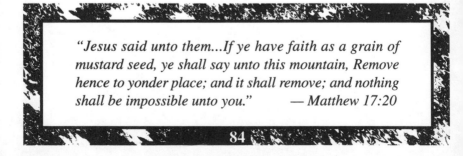

"Jesus said unto them...If ye have faith as a grain of mustard seed, ye shall say unto this mountain, Remove hence to yonder place; and it shall remove; and nothing shall be impossible unto you." — Matthew 17:20

Needing Mustard Seed Faith

Jesus, I need mustard seed faith.
    I lack the trust to start small.
        I look for big harvests before I ever sow.
            I seek major miracles before I believe for little ones.

Teach me, Master, to trust You in the little things;
        That I might be proved faithful and able to receive
        greater things.

Lord, to me, even the possible at times seems impossible.
        Plant within me mustard seed faith;
        That I might move both molehills and mountains.

Amen.

In the Words of Wigglesworth...

"As the day of the Lord hastens on we need to walk by faith until overcoming all things by our simple belief in Jesus Christ; we walk right into glory."

Believe! The Way to Overcome, p. 2

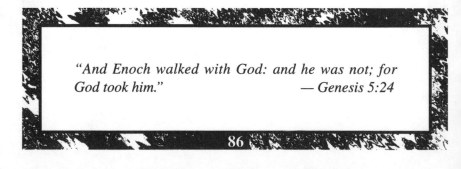

"And Enoch walked with God: and he was not; for God took him." — *Genesis 5:24*

Walk With God

Lord, how I long to walk with You.

I pray for walking that leads to talking,

And talking that leads to sharing,

And sharing that leads to intimacy,

And intimacy that leads to glory,

And glory leading to glory upon glory.

Teach me to walk with You, O Lord,

So that my walk will imprint in Your footsteps,

And my life might be totally taken by Yours.

Amen.

In the Words of Wigglesworth...

"For God has not accomplished something in us that should lie dormant, but He has brought within us a power, a revelation, a life so great that I believe God wants to reveal the greatness of it. The possibilities of man in the hands of God! There isn't anything you can imagine greater than what the man may accomplish."

Christ in Us, p. 2

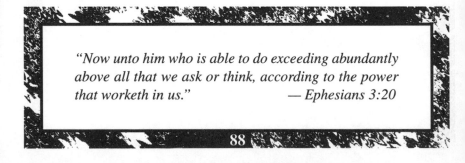

"Now unto him who is able to do exceeding abundantly above all that we ask or think, according to the power that worketh in us." — Ephesians 3:20

Dormant No Longer

Creator of the universe,

Thy possibilities within me are infinite —

Beyond all my imaginations,

Crossing the lines of my every limit,

Exceeding my wildest expectations.

Therefore, don't do what I ask,

Rather, do that which is so far beyond me that I cannot even
begin to know what to ask, think, imagine, feel or do.

Exceed my everything with Thine all in all. Amen.

In the Words of Wigglesworth...

"I have looked through my Bible, and I cannot find where God brings disease and sickness. I know there is glory, and I know it is the power of God that brings the glory. It isn't God at all, but the devil that brings sickness and disease."

Christ in Us, p. 10

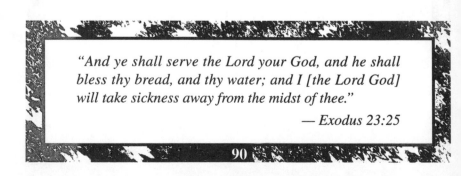

"And ye shall serve the Lord your God, and he shall bless thy bread, and thy water; and I [the Lord God] will take sickness away from the midst of thee."

— Exodus 23:25

From Whence Come Sickness and Disease?

Jesus,
I know that by Your stripes I am healed.

For whence comes disease?
> Chasten me not by allowing the enemy to attack nor
> my sin to devastate me.
>> From Your hand alone comes every healing touch.

Touch me, Lord.
> Heal me.
>> Save me.

Take away every disease from the midst of my life.
> Great Physician, heal me that I might declare Thy
> glory. Amen.

In the Words of Wigglesworth...

"The reason the world is not seeing Jesus is because Christians are not filled with Jesus. They are satisfied with weekly meetings, occasionally reading the Bible and sometimes praying. Beloved, if God lays hold of you by the Spirit, you will find that there is an end of everything and a beginning of God, so that your whole body becomes seasoned with a divine likeness of God."

Divine Life Brings Divine Health, p. 1

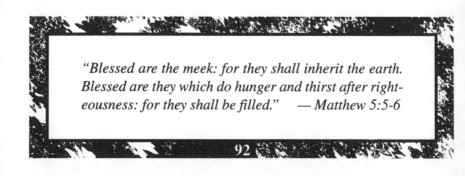

"Blessed are the meek: for they shall inherit the earth. Blessed are they which do hunger and thirst after righteousness: for they shall be filled." — Matthew 5:5-6

Lord, I've Been Too Satisfied

Lord, I've been too satisfied of late with my own efforts,
   Feeling good about going to church,
      Feeling proud about my giving,
         Feeling righteous about my good works,
            Feeling pure by abstaining from impurity,
               Feeling holy by separating from the world.

Lord, something haunts my inner being,
   Stirring an uneasiness within my soul.

Could it be that my satisfaction portends danger to my spirit
and peril to my soul?
      Sound the alarm within me, Holy Spirit.
      Disturb me with the awesome sense of Your Presence.
         Appall me with the reality of my sin.
            Stir me with a dissatisfaction for all that the
               world satisfies in me,

Perplex me with Your mystery,
   So that I will never believe I have all the answers.

Lord God, shatter my satisfaction
   With an unending hunger and thirst for You. Amen.

In the Words of Wigglesworth...

"I pray God will give us a way out of difficulties, and a way into rest. The writer of Hebrews tells us that there remaineth a rest to the people of God, and they which have entered into that rest have ceased from their own works. O, what a blessed state of rest that is, to cease from your own works; where God is now enthroned on your life, and you are working for Him by a new order, instead of struggling in the old ways."

Divine Life Brings Divine Health, p. 3

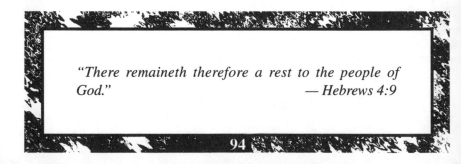

"There remaineth therefore a rest to the people of God." — Hebrews 4:9

Rest

Jesus, bid me come unto Thee;

For I am tired and heavy laden.

I yearn for Thy rest.

Hold me in Thy arms.

Put my head on Thy bosom.

Whisper to me Thy words of comfort.

Soothe my aching body and soul;

Refresh my spirit;

My toils I lay at Thy feet.

Thou alone art my rest. Amen.

In the Words of Wigglesworth...

"You must give God your life. You must see that sickness has to go and God has to come in: that your lives have to be clean, and God will keep you holy."

Divine Life Brings Divine Health, p. 5

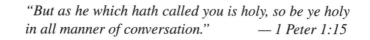

"But as he which hath called you is holy, so be ye holy in all manner of conversation."   — *1 Peter 1:15*

Holiness

Sovereign God, I know that holiness is not optional, but I
find myself compromising too often.
> I catch myself trying to walk too close to the edge
> between holiness and the world.
>> I discover partial truths becoming my defense,
>> Excuses becoming my covering,
>> Rationalizations substituting for revelations,
And good ideas replacing God ideas in my daily decisions.

Jesus, save me from myself for nothing I do can make me holy.
> Save me from my compromises, defenses,
> rationalizations and good ideas.

Holy Spirit, only Your holiness can make me holy.
> I am sick of being sick,
>> Tired of being tired,
>>> Fed up with being fed up;
>>>> So purify that all dross might be consumed.
Spirit of God, make me holy as You are Holy. Clean me up.
Wash me through. Amen.

In the Words of Wigglesworth...

"Purity is bold. The more pure, the more bold you are. God wants to bring us into that divine purity of heart and life, that holy boldness; not self-righteousness, but a pure, holy, divine appointment by One who will come in and live with you, defying the power of Satan and standing you in a place of victory, overcoming the world."

Divine Life Brings Divine Health, p. 6

"Keep thyself pure." — *1 Timothy 5:22*

Purify My Heart

God, purify my heart.

Examine every thought.

Cleanse every desire.

Scour each passion.

Purge all hidden sin.

Make me bold for Jesus.

Defying Satan's power,

Standing in the place of victory,

I overcome Satan in Jesus' name.

God, purify my heart.

Amen.

In the Words of Wigglesworth...

"When the Spirit of God comes into your body, He will transform you and quicken you. O, there is a life in the Spirit which makes you free from the law of sin and death, and there is an audacity about it — also there's a personality about it. It is the personality of the Deity. It is God in you."

Divine Life Brings Divine Health, p. 6

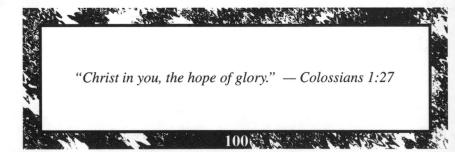

"Christ in you, the hope of glory." — *Colossians 1:27*

Christ in Me

Christ, indwell me.

Transform me.

Live in me with Your Spirit.

Free me from the law of sin and death.

Quicken me.

Embolden me.

Exude Your personality through me.

God in Christ Jesus by Your Holy Spirit,

Indwell me.

Amen.

In the Words of Wigglesworth...

"Without the cross, without Christ's righteousness, without the new birth, without the indwelling Christ, without this divine incoming of God, I see myself as a failure. But God, the Holy Ghost, can come in and take our place till we are renewed in righteousness, made the children of God, the sons of God. Do you think that God would make you to be a failure?

God has never made man to be a failure. So, when I look at you I know that there is a capability that can be put into you which has the capacity of controlling and bringing everything into subjection. Yes, there is the capacity of the power of Christ to dwell in you, to bring every evil thing under you till you can put your feet upon it and be master of the flesh and the devil."

Divine Life Brings Divine Health, p. 7

"Nay, in all these things we are more than conquerors through him that loved us." — Romans 8:37

Not a Failure

In You, O Christ,
> I am not a failure.
> Your cross won my victory.
> Your new birth renewed my personality.
>> Your righteousness purchased my salvation.
>> Your indwelling made me a new creation.
> Through Your capacity I have veracity,
> Through Your control I can captain my soul.

In You, O Christ,
> I put every evil under my feet,
> I conquer every devil I meet;
> I master the flesh;
> I uncover every sin to confess.
>> I receive Your healing;
>> I feel what You are feeling.

In You, O Christ,
> I am more than a conqueror. Amen.

In the Words of Wigglesworth...

"Through the revelation of the Word of God we find that divine healing is solely for the glory of God, and salvation is to make you to know you have to be inhabited by another, even God, and you have to walk with God in newness of life."

Divine Life Brings Divine Health, p. 8.

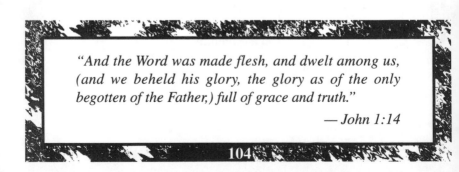

"And the Word was made flesh, and dwelt among us, (and we beheld his glory, the glory as of the only begotten of the Father,) full of grace and truth."

— John 1:14

Healed for His Glory

Pour Thy healing in me.

Glorify Thyself in me.

Reveal Thy truth in me.

Live Thy life in me.

Have Thy way in me.

Walk Thy walk in me.

Renew Thy newness in me.

Amen.

In the Words of Wigglesworth...

"The people in whom God delights are the ones who rest upon His Word without wavering. So only believe! Only believe! All things are possible — only believe!"

Extraordinary, p. 1

"As soon as Jesus heard the word that was spoken, he saith unto the ruler of the synagogue, Be not afraid, only believe." — Mark 5:36

Only Believe

Lord, I am not afraid.

Help me to only believe.

Amen.

In the Words of Wigglesworth...

"God never intended His people to be ordinary or common-place. His intentions were that they should be on fire for Him, conscious of His divine power, realizing the glory of the cross that foreshadows the crown."

Extraordinary, pp. 1-2

"Blessed is the man that endureth temptation: for when he is tried, he shall receive the crown of life, which the Lord hath promised to them that love him."

— James 1:12

Not Ordinary

Lord, help me to be extraordinary,

To leave behind the commonplace for the fireplace;

To blaze with Your glory;

To receive the crown of life;

To proclaim for eternity the wonder of Your cross.

Amen.

In the Words of Wigglesworth...

"God has privileged us in Christ Jesus to live above the ordinary plane of human life. Those who want to be ordinary and live on a lower plane, can do so. But as for me, I will not! For the same unction, the same zeal, the same Holy Ghost power is at our command as was at the command of Stephen and the apostles."

Extraordinary, p. 2

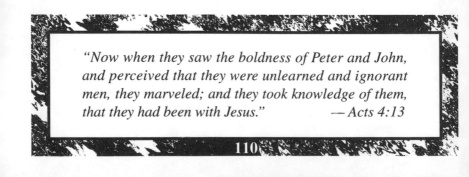

"Now when they saw the boldness of Peter and John, and perceived that they were unlearned and ignorant men, they marveled; and they took knowledge of them, that they had been with Jesus." — Acts 4:13

Boldness From Jesus

God,

May I exhibit the same boldness
as those first apostles,

Not gaining confidence from my knowledge
nor my achievements,

Rather, may I impress others not with what I know,

But with whom I live — Jesus!

Amen.

In the Words of Wigglesworth...

"Now a lively hope is exactly opposite to dead, exactly opposite to normal. Lively hope is movement. Lively hope is looking into, pressing into, leaving everything behind you. Lively hope is keeping the vision. Lively hope sees Him coming. You are not trying to make yourself feel that you are believing, but the lively hope is filled with the joy of the expectation of the King!"

Rising Into the Heavenlies, p. 6

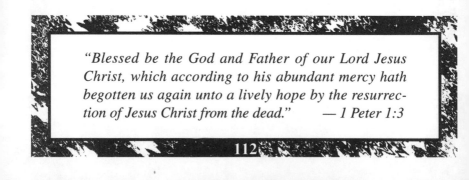

"Blessed be the God and Father of our Lord Jesus Christ, which according to his abundant mercy hath begotten us again unto a lively hope by the resurrection of Jesus Christ from the dead." — 1 Peter 1:3

Lively Hope

Jesus,

My hope is built on nothing less than Thy blood and
   righteousness.
Be Thou my hope when darkness begins to fall.
Be Thou my hope when expectations wane.
Be Thou my hope when I fail to hear Thy call.
Be Thou my hope when life is filled with pains.
Be Thou my lively hope.

Jesus,

Thou art my hope for looking into heaven.
Thou art my hope for pressing into Thy throne.
Thou art my hope for leaving this world behind and
   following Thee.
Thou art my hope for dreams and visions.
Thou art my hope for seeing Thy coming.
Thou art my hope not my feeling hopeful.
Thou art my joy not my feeling happy.

Jesus,

Thou alone art my lively hope. Amen.

In the Words of Wigglesworth...

"Beloved, as you are tested in the fire, the Master is cleaning away all that cannot bring out His image, cleaning away all the dross from your life and every evil power, till He sees His face right in your life."

Rising Into the Heavenlies, p. 5

"Every man's work shall be made manifest: for the day shall declare it, because it shall be revealed by fire; and the fire shall try every man's work of what sort it is." — 1 Corinthians 3:13

Tested in the Fire

Master, test me in the fire.

Clean away all that does not reflect You.

Burn away the temporal.

Bring every evil thought and intent low.

When I look into the mirror of my life,
my one desire is to see You. Amen.

In the Words of Wigglesworth...

"We are glad for cathedrals and churches, but God does not dwell in temples made by hands, but in the fleshly tables of the heart. Here is true worship. God is a Spirit, and they that worship Him must worship in Spirit and in truth. The church is the body of Christ. Its worship is a heart worship. He will give us that place of worship. How my heart cries out for a living faith with a deep vision of God."

Now! Now! Now!, p. 1

"Know ye not that your body is the temple of the Holy Ghost which is in you...For ye are bought with a price: therefore glorify God in your body; and in your spirit, which are God's." — 1 Corinthians 6:19-20

The Temple

Holy Spirit,

Deposit Yourself within me;

That I might be Your sanctuary,

Filled with Your Spirit,

Alive with Your power,

Worshiping God in Spirit and in truth,

Overflowing with a deep faith.

Grant me the vision of myself as Your temple.

Amen.

In the Words of Wigglesworth...

"You are in a good place when you weep before God, repenting over the least thing. When everything is wrong, you cry unto the Lord! It is when we are close to God that our hearts are revealed."

Now! Now! Now!, p. 3

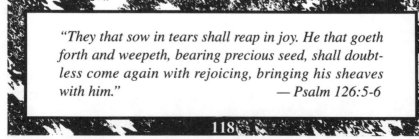

"They that sow in tears shall reap in joy. He that goeth forth and weepeth, bearing precious seed, shall doubtless come again with rejoicing, bringing his sheaves with him." — *Psalm 126:5-6*

Sowing in Tears

God, I weep whenever I enter Your presence.
My tears are for my sin, and not mine alone,
but the sins of Your people and of this world.
Let each tear that I sow be a washing by Your Spirit.
Let each tear I sow be a time of breaking.
Let each tear I sow be for souls lost and my reluctance
to harvest.
Let each tear I sow be for each unkind word I say,
each mean look I give,
each cruel act I commit,
each hateful thought I have,
each fleshly passion I desire.

Jesus, I pour my tears upon Your feet.
Anoint me with the fellowship of Your sufferings,
with the joy of the cross,
with the tribulations of serving You.
Anoint me with the oil of Your Spirit so that I might
always weep over sin and never grieve You. Amen.

In the Words of Wigglesworth...

"When God speaks, it is a nail in a sure place."

Now! Now! Now!, p. 5

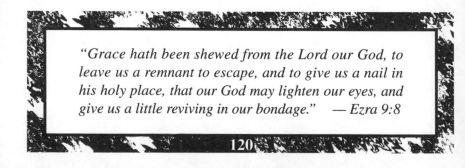

"Grace hath been shewed from the Lord our God, to leave us a remnant to escape, and to give us a nail in his holy place, that our God may lighten our eyes, and give us a little reviving in our bondage." — Ezra 9:8

A Nail in a Sure Place

Jesus,

Nail me to Your cross.

Pierce my heart with Your love.

Fix my eyes on You.

Anchor me to You so that in life's storms

You will be my safe harbor,

You will be my guiding light,

You will the be the sure place of my refuge.

Amen.

In the Words of Wigglesworth...

"God wants you to have a living faith now, to get a vital touch, shaking the foundation of all weakness. When you were saved, you were saved the moment you believed, and you will be healed the moment you believe."

Is Anyone Sick?, p. 5

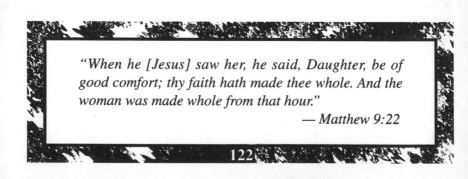

"When he [Jesus] saw her, he said, Daughter, be of good comfort; thy faith hath made thee whole. And the woman was made whole from that hour."

— Matthew 9:22

Believe and Be Healed!

Jesus, I need Thy touch.
    Shake my weakness.
        Break my infirmity.
            Destroy my disease.

Jesus, touch me, heal me.
    I believe:
        You are my healing,
           my wholeness,
              my health,
                my strength,
                    my salvation.

Sickness, be gone in the name of Jesus. Amen.

In the Words of Wigglesworth...

"If you build on anything else but the Word of God — on imagination, or sentimentality, or any feelings, or any special joy — it will mean nothing unless you have a foundation which is the Word of God."

Faith (Part One), p. 2

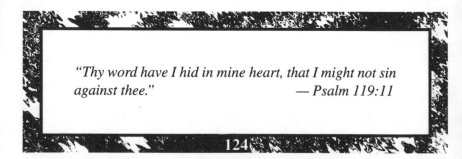

"Thy word have I hid in mine heart, that I might not sin against thee." — *Psalm 119:11*

The Foundation of God's Word

God, I have sought to build my life
   on what I imagine,
      on what feels good,
         on sentiment and wishfulness,
            on fleeting happiness that comes in
               momentary pleasure.

Wreck my building.
   Destroy my foundations.
      Build me upon Your Word.
         That is enough. Amen.

In the Words of Wigglesworth...

"Beloved, don't forget that every day must be a day of advancement. If you have not made any advancement since yesterday, in a measure you are a backslider. There is only one way for you between Calvary and the glory. It is forward. It is every day forward. It is no day going back."

Faith (Part One), p. 5

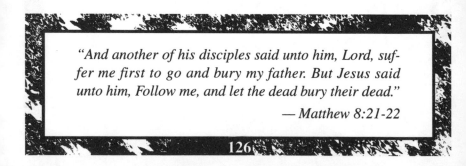

"And another of his disciples said unto him, Lord, suffer me first to go and bury my father. But Jesus said unto him, Follow me, and let the dead bury their dead."

— Matthew 8:21-22

Nothing to Go Back for

Jesus,

I confess there's nothing to go back for,

No memory too precious,

No obligation too important,

No tradition too sacred,

No treasure too cherished,

To go back for.

I refuse to go back.

Going forward with You is the only direction I seek.

Grant me the courage to release the past,

To place my future in Your hands,

And to grasp the moment by holding tightly to You.

Amen.

In the Words of Wigglesworth...

"When you think there is no hope for you, and you have passed everything, that is the time God makes the man. When tried by fire, God purges you, takes away the dross, and brings forth pure gold. Only melted gold is minted.

Only moistened clay receives the mold. Only softened wax receives the seal. Only broken, contrite hearts receive the mark as the Potter turns us on His wheel, shaped and burnt to take and keep the heavenly mold, the stamp of God's seal in pure gold."

Faith (Part One), p. 5

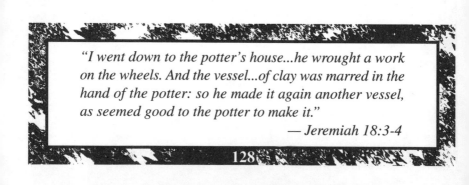

"I went down to the potter's house...he wrought a work on the wheels. And the vessel...of clay was marred in the hand of the potter: so he made it again another vessel, as seemed good to the potter to make it."

— Jeremiah 18:3-4

On the Potter's Wheel

Willing, Lord, I place myself in Your hands,

Be the Potter of my life.

Break me.

Shape me.

Mold me.

Fill me.

Use me.

With the water of Your Spirit,

Keep me as soft, pliable clay in Your hands.

Amen.

In the Words of Wigglesworth...

"I believe that there is only one way to all the treasures of God, and it is the way of faith. There is only one principle underlying all the attributes and all the beatitudes of the mighty ascension into the glories of Christ, and it is by faith. All the promises are yea and amen to them that believe."

Faith (Part Two), p. 1

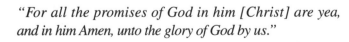

"For all the promises of God in him [Christ] are yea, and in him Amen, unto the glory of God by us."

— 2 Corinthians 1:20

Yea and Amen

Christ,

By faith I claim all Your promises to be

Yea and amen

In me.

Amen.

In the Words of Wigglesworth...

"Prayer changes hearts, but it never changes God. God is the same yesterday, today and forever — full of love, full of entreaty, full of helpfulness."

Faith (Part Two), p. 2

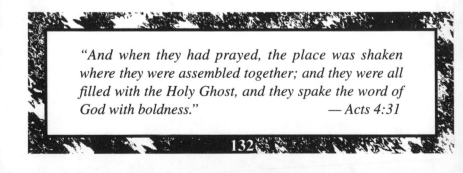

"And when they had prayed, the place was shaken where they were assembled together; and they were all filled with the Holy Ghost, and they spake the word of God with boldness." — Acts 4:31

Change My Heart

This prayer, O Lord, is not an entreaty to change You,
Rather, I seek to have You shake me,
Fill me with the Holy Ghost,
Help and love me.
Make me bold to speak Your Word.

O God, You are the immovable, immutable One who sustains all things.
Change my heart that its stone might be crushed;
That I may be shaken as salt into the world. Amen.

In the Words of Wigglesworth...

"You can never live if you have never been dead. You must die if you want to live."

Faith (Part Two), p. 6

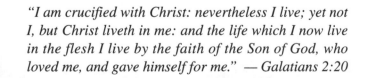

"I am crucified with Christ: nevertheless I live; yet not I, but Christ liveth in me: and the life which I now live in the flesh I live by the faith of the Son of God, who loved me, and gave himself for me." — Galatians 2:20

Dying to Live

Christ,

I'm dying to live in You.

Amen.

In the Words of Wigglesworth...

"Oh, beloved, God is a real essence of joy to us in a time that seems barren, when nothing can help us but the light from heaven far above the brightness of the sun."

Our Calling (Part One), p. 2

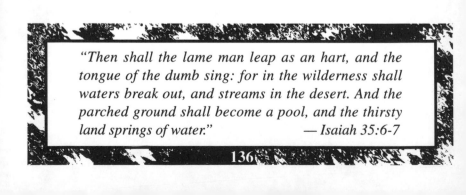

"Then shall the lame man leap as an hart, and the tongue of the dumb sing: for in the wilderness shall waters break out, and streams in the desert. And the parched ground shall become a pool, and the thirsty land springs of water." — Isaiah 35:6-7

Rain on My Desert

God,

Rain Your joy upon the parched,
barren desert of my soul.

The soil of my life so needs to soak
in Your rain and light.

Grow within me a tree of life.

Graft me to the vine of Your Son.

Produce fruit in me by Your Spirit.

Let me flower with the sweet perfume
of Your fragrance.

Be in me a river of living water
to irrigate the desert within and without.

Amen.

In the Words of Wigglesworth...

"Keep men's eyes off you, but get their eyes on the Lord. Live in the world without a touch or taint of any natural thing moving you. Live high in the order and authority of God, and see that everything is bearing you on to greater heights and depths and greater knowledge of the love of God."

Our Calling (Part One), p. 4

"Let thine eyes look right on, and let thine eyelids look straight before thee." — Proverbs 4:25

Eyes Only for Jesus

Lord, remove pride and arrogance from my life. When others see me, give them eyes for only You. Remove the expectation of being noticed from my heart. When others fail to notice or thank me, empower me to thank You.

Help me to seek my affirmation and acceptance from You and not from man. Create in me a desire to please You and not to seek the approval of others. May my only credentials be the cross, the blood and the Word.

How I desire to live high in Your order and authority forsaking worldly ways and power for godliness. The knowledge of You and Your love will take me to the greatest heights and through the deepest depths of my life.

Spirit of God, give me eyes only for You. Amen.

In the Words of Wigglesworth...

"Virtue is always manifested through blessings which you have passed on. Nothing will be of any importance to you except that which you pass on to others. God wants us to be filled with perfumes of holy incense that we may be poured out for others and that others may receive the graces of the Spirit."

Our Calling (Part Two), p. 1

"The righteous giveth and spareth not."

— Proverbs 21:26

Lord, Bless Me to...

Lord, bless me to be a blessing.

Fill me to be a fountain.

Use me to be a vessel.

Pour me into the lives of others.

Heal me to be a healing.

Forgive me to forgive.

Prosper me to prosper others.

Thank You, Lord, for teaching me the joy of generosity.

So that I might give to others all that You've given me.

Amen.

In the Words of Wigglesworth...

"But oh, the baptism of the Holy Ghost! The baptism of fire! The baptism of power! The baptism of oneness! The baptism of communion! The baptism of the Spirit of Life takes the man, shakes him through, builds him up and makes him know he is a new creature in the Spirit, worshiping God in the Spirit."

Our Calling (Part Two), p. 4

"He [Jesus] shall baptize you with the Holy Ghost, and with fire." — Matthew 3:11

Baptize Me!

Jesus,

Baptize me with the fire of the Holy Ghost,

Take me.

Shake me.

Make me a new creation.

Set me ablaze with Your Spirit

That like the burning bush of old,

So that others might seek You out

And stand on holy ground.

Amen.

In the Words of Wigglesworth...

"The church will rise to the highest position when there is no schism in the body on the lines of unbelief. When we all, with one heart and one faith, believe the Word as it is spoken, then signs and wonders and divers miracles will be manifested everywhere."

Our Calling (Part Two), p. 5

"There is one body, and one Spirit, even as ye are called in one hope of your calling; One Lord, one faith, one baptism, One God and Father of all, who is above all." — *Ephesians 4:4-6*

One Body

Christ,

Make Your church one body.

Heal every schism.

Bind us together in love;

Build us in one faith.

Knit us together in one heart.

Manifest in Your body signs, wonders and miracles.

Amen.

In the Words of Wigglesworth...

"God has never been able to make goodness except out of our helplessness lest we should glorify through the flesh. God destroys every line of flesh that no flesh can glory in His sight. If we have any glory, we will glory in the Lord."

Our Calling (Part Two), p. 7

"There is none that doeth good, no, not one."

— Romans 3:12

Glory in the Lord

Lord, if there be any praise,

If there be any glory,

If there be any recognition,

If there be any success,

If there be any prosperity,

If there be any victory,

If there be any glory,

Let it all go to You.

Amen.

In the Words of Wigglesworth...

"Who knows how to pray but as the Spirit prayeth? What kind of prayer does the Spirit pray? The Spirit always brings to your remembrance the mind of the Scriptures and brings forth all your cry and your need better than your own words. The Spirit always takes the Word of God and brings your heart, mind, soul, cry and need into the presence of God."

Ye Are Our Epistle (Part One), p. 2

"Likewise the Spirit also helpeth our infirmities: for we know not what we should pray for as we ought: but the Spirit itself maketh intercession for us with groanings which cannot be uttered."   — Romans 8:26

The Spirit Praying in Me

Holy Spirit,

Bring to mind the Word.

Pray the Word in me,

Through me,

For me.

Holy Spirit, pray in me.

Amen.

In the Words of Wigglesworth...

"When God gets into the depths of our hearts, He purifies every intention of the thoughts and joys."

Ye Are Our Epistle (Part One), p. 3

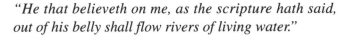

"He that believeth on me, as the scripture hath said, out of his belly shall flow rivers of living water."

— John 7:38

Purify Me

Father,

Purify me deep within, that out of me might flow
rivers of living water.

Amen.

In the Words of Wigglesworth...

"We want to get to a place where we are beyond trusting in ourselves. Beloved, there is such failure in self-assurances. It is not bad to have good things on the lines of satisfaction, but we must never have anything human that we rest upon. There is only one sure place of rest — trusting in God."

Ye Are Our Epistle (Part One), p. 3

"For we walk by faith, not by sight."

— 2 Corinthians 5:7

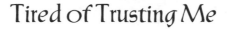

Tired of Trusting Me

Jesus, I'm tired of trusting me.
    Help me get beyond myself to a place where there is
        only Thee.

Jesus, I'm tired of trusting me.
    Help me get beyond my bondages to a place that's
        really free.

Jesus, I'm tired of trusting me.
    Help me be assured by faith and not what I see.

Jesus, I'm tired of trusting me.
    You're the place of rest where I always want to be.

Amen.

In the Words of Wigglesworth...

"Every day must be a revival touch in our hearts. Every day must change us after His fashion."

That I May Know Him, p. 3

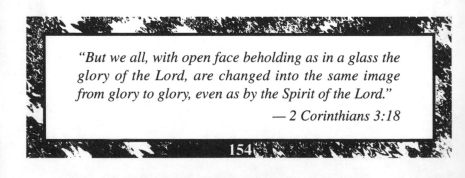

"But we all, with open face beholding as in a glass the glory of the Lord, are changed into the same image from glory to glory, even as by the Spirit of the Lord."

— 2 Corinthians 3:18

Change Me

Christ,

Change me to be like You,

In mind, heart, soul and spirit.

No change I make ever lasts.

Lasting change abides in You.

Change me, Christ, to image You in all I do.

Amen.

In the Words of Wigglesworth...

"Never take advantage of the Holy Ghost, but allow the Holy Ghost to take advantage of you. Once I thought I possessed the Holy Ghost, but I have come to the conclusion that He has to be entirely the possessor of me."

God Bless You, p. 11

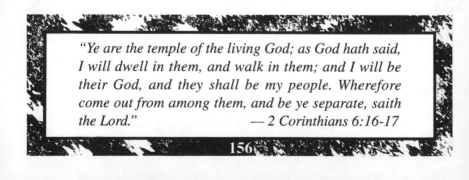

"Ye are the temple of the living God; as God hath said, I will dwell in them, and walk in them; and I will be their God, and they shall be my people. Wherefore come out from among them, and be ye separate, saith the Lord." — 2 Corinthians 6:16-17

Possess Me

All that I own owns me.

I surrender all.

So now, possess me, Holy Spirit.

Take advantage of me.

Be Thou the possessor of me.

Amen.

In the Words of Wigglesworth...

"The greatest blessing that can come to you will be that the Word of life in going forth will inwardly create in you a deeper desire for God. As the Spirit of God is giving you the Word, it will make you long more for God, more the holiness of God, more for the righteousness of God, for He has to make you this day to know that as He is pure, you have to be pure."

Sons of God, p. 2

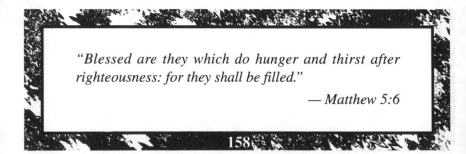

"Blessed are they which do hunger and thirst after righteousness: for they shall be filled."

— Matthew 5:6

Hunger

Satisfier of my inner desire,

I hunger for Thy righteousness.
I thirst for Thy living water.

I hunger for Thy bread of life.
I thirst for Thy new wine.

I hunger for the meat of Thy Word.
I thirst for flowing rivers of holiness and power.

My deepest, inner desire is for purity.
I hunger and thirst for Thee.

Amen.

In the Words of Wigglesworth...

"You will find that whatever work you have to do will be made easier if you keep your mind stayed on the Lord. Blessed is the man that has his mind stayed upon the Lord! We must see to it that in the world we are not moved."

Sons of God, p. 6

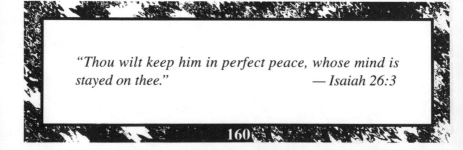

"Thou wilt keep him in perfect peace, whose mind is stayed on thee." — Isaiah 26:3

Stayed Upon Thee

Lord,

Keep me in perfect peace
as my mind is stayed upon Thee.

Amen.

In the Words of Wigglesworth...

"Faith is an act. Faith is a leap. Faith jumps in. Faith claims. Faith has an author. Faith's author is Jesus. He is the author and the finisher of faith."

Sons of God, p. 13

"Looking unto Jesus the author and finisher of our faith." — *Hebrews 12:2*

Faith Acts

Jesus, by faith I will act.

I will take the leap of faith.

I will jump whenever You call.

I will claim Your every promise.

I will trust You to author and finish my faith.

Jesus, give me the gift of faith!

Amen.

In the Words of Wigglesworth...

"How much dare you ask for? How much dare you think? How much dare you expect to come? How much? May I move you to the banquet, this treasure place, this much more, this abundant, this abounding, this exceedingly more? Jump into God. Dare to believe. Faith is enough. Ask and believe."

Sons of God, p. 13

"I am come that they might have life, and that they might have it more abundantly."   — *John 10:10*

Praying With Daring

Jesus,

Teach me to be daring when I pray.

Teach me to be daring when I think.

Sit me at Your banquet table.

Feed me the feast of Your bread and wine.

I claim exceedingly more than I can think or imagine.

Expand my visions and dreams

That I might walk in Your abundance.

Amen.

In the Words of Wigglesworth...

"The greatest plan that Jesus ever showed forth in His ministry was the ministry of service. He said, 'I am amongst you as one that serveth.' And when we come to a place where we serve for pure love's sake because it is the divine hand of the Master on us, we shall find out that we shall never fail."

A teaching on Ephesians 4:1-16, p. 2

"For whether is greater, he that sitteth at meat, or he that serveth? is not he that sitteth at meat? but I am among you as he that serveth." — Luke 22:27

To Serve

Lord Jesus,
    I ask for Your mind, Your attitude of serving.
        Cultivate in me the desire to serve others simply
        for love's sake.
            Humble me.
Teach me how to descend into greatness.
From last place show me how to be great.
As a servant, teach me how to lead.
Like Joseph, take me from pit to pinnacle.
    Open my eyes to the least of these — the sick,
    lonely, imprisoned, naked and hungry.
        Even as You have served me from the cross,
    Enable me to take up my cross and serve others
    for Your name's sake. Amen.

In the Words of Wigglesworth...

"The devil has nothing against you, but the devil is against the living Christ and wants to destroy Him. If you are filled with the living Christ, the devil is anxious to get you out of the way, thereby destroying Christ's power in you. Say this, 'Now, Lord, look after this property of yours.' Then the devil cannot get near."

A teaching on Ephesians 4:1-16, p. 10

"Ye belong to Christ." — Mark 9:41

The Lord's Property

Lord, I belong to You.

Now, Lord, look after this property of Yours.

Can't touch me, Satan.

Can't touch my family, my church, my friends,
my property, my life.

I belong to Jesus.

Now, Lord, look after Your property.

Amen.

In the Words of Wigglesworth...

"I want to stir you up today. If I cannot make a diseased person that is suffering righteously indignant against that place, I cannot help him. If I can make every sufferer know that suffering, disease and all evil are the workings of the devil, I can help him."

The Glory of the Incorruptible, p. 10

"The thief cometh not, but for to steal, and to kill, and to destroy." — John 10:10

Destroying the Works
of the Thief

O Lord, move away disease,
    Move away blind eyes,
        Move away imperfect vision.

Give the Word.
Let us understand the blood and the spirit of prophecy and
testimony.

Let us understand, O God, that Thou art still building the
foundation on the prophets,
    And on the apostles,
        And on all that worketh Thy wonderful Word.

So build us till every soul is filled with divine grace. Amen.

In the Words of Wigglesworth...

"It is not to tell what God has for you in the future. Press in and claim your rights. Let the Lord Jesus be so glorified that He will make you a fruit bearer, strong in power, giving glory to God, having no confidence in the flesh but being separated from natural things living now in the Spirit, living fully in the will of God."

A teaching on Ephesians 4:1-16, p. 10

"Herein is my Father glorified, that ye bear much fruit; so shall ye be my disciples."   — *John 15:8*

Confident Prayer

Jesus, my confidence is in You.

My flesh fails me.

My ideas fade away.

My success disappears.

My future appears uncertain.

I press in to claim what You have promised.

Make of me a fruit bearer,

Strong in power,

Glorifying You,

Living fully in Your will.

Amen.

In the Words of Wigglesworth...

"Let the Spirit cover you so that you may be intensely in earnest about the deep things of God. You should be so in the order of the Spirit that you may know that your will, mind and heart is so centered in God. You should be so centered that He may lift you into the pavilion of splendor where you hear His voice; lift you to the place where the breath of the Almighty can send you to pray and to preach having His Spirit upon you."

Temptation Endured, p. 1

"He shall cover thee with his feathers, and under his wings shalt thou trust: his truth shall be thy shield and buckler." — *Psalm 91:4*

Cover Me, Holy Spirit

Cover me, Holy Spirit.
> Make me intensely earnest about the deep things of
> God.
> Reveal to me Your will.
> Put within me the mind of Christ.
> Center my heart on the Father.
> Lift me into the pavilion of splendor that I may hear
> Your voice.

Breathe on me, Holy Spirit.
> Send me to the secret place of prayer.
> Preach through me the Word You desire to be spoken.
> Cover me, Holy Spirit, with Your wings.

Amen.

In the Words of Wigglesworth...

"When you are in prayer, remember how near you are to the Lord. It is a time God wants you to change strength there, and He wants you to remember He is with you."

Workers Together With God, p. 4

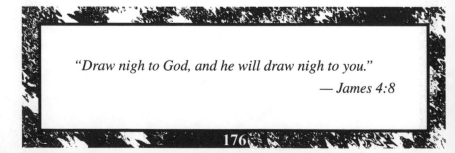

"Draw nigh to God, and he will draw nigh to you."

— James 4:8

Drawing Near to God

Father,

I am drawing near to Thee,

Claiming Thy promise,

That Thou wilt draw near to me.

Amen.

In the Words of Wigglesworth...

"You must every day make higher ground. You must deny yourself to go with God. God wants you pure in heart. He wants your intense desire after holiness."

Workers Together With God, p. 5

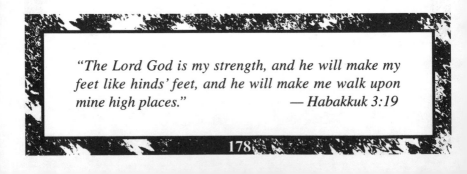

"The Lord God is my strength, and he will make my feet like hinds' feet, and he will make me walk upon mine high places." — *Habakkuk 3:19*

Higher Ground

Today, Lord,

Take me to higher ground.

Set my feet on the high places.

I deny myself that I might go on with You.

Purify my heart.

Fill me with an intense desire for Your holiness.

Lord, take me higher than I've ever been before.

Amen.

In the Words of Wigglesworth...

"If you are in His love, you will be swallowed up with holy desire. You will desire only the Lord. Your mind will be filled with divine reflection. Your whole heart will be taken up with the things that pertain to the kingdom of God. You will live in the secret place of the Most High, and you will abide there."

A teaching on 2 Corinthians 3, p. 16

"He that dwelleth in the secret place of the most High shall abide under the shadow of the Almighty."

— Psalm 91:1

Dwell in God's Secret Place

O Most High,

How I love Thee!

How I long to dwell in Thy secret place,

Filled with divine reflection of Thee.

Swallow me up with holy desire.

Reign in my heart as King.

Abide in me that I might abide eternally in Thee.

Amen.

In the Words of Wigglesworth...

"God comes to you and says, 'Behold, you are sons of God!' Oh, that we could have a regiment rising, claiming their rights, standing erect with a holy vision and full of inward power, saying, 'I am, by the grace of God, a son of God!'"

Sons of God, p. 7.

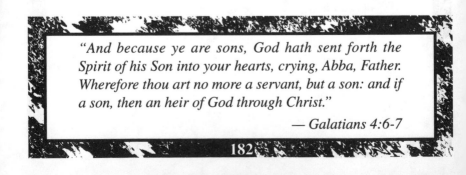

"And because ye are sons, God hath sent forth the Spirit of his Son into your hearts, crying, Abba, Father. Wherefore thou art no more a servant, but a son: and if a son, then an heir of God through Christ."

— *Galatians 4:6-7*

I Am a Son of God

I have no right in and of myself to be part of Thy family,

But in Thy good pleasure,

Thou hast adopted me.

Thou hast given me Thy name

And surrounded me with Thy family.

I stand erect bearing no shame for the name I bear is

The name above all names.

By Thy grace,
I declare to all the hosts of heaven above

And to all the demons of hell below that:

"I am, by the grace of God, a son of God!"

Abba, Father, how I love Thee.

Amen.

In the Words of Wigglesworth...

"Let Christ have His perfect work. You must cease to be. That is a difficult thing for you and me but is not trouble at all when you are in the hands of the Potter. You are only wrong when you are kicking. You are all right when you are still and He is forming you afresh. So let Him form you afresh today and make of you a vessel that will stand the stress."

Temptation Endured, p. 7.

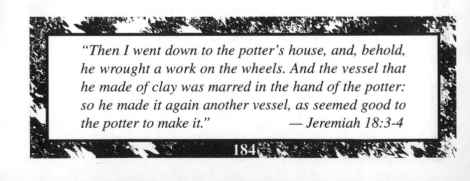

"Then I went down to the potter's house, and, behold, he wrought a work on the wheels. And the vessel that he made of clay was marred in the hand of the potter: so he made it again another vessel, as seemed good to the potter to make it." — Jeremiah 18:3-4

Mold Me

Lord, how hard it is to stay still.

Your shaping goes contrary to my expectations.

The sculpture You envision me to be
is quite unlike my own projections.

And when You break what is unyielded in me,

I cry out in selfish remorse
desiring my own image over Yours.

I need to be formed afresh today.

Yesterday's shape serves poorly for today's service.

So make of me a vessel

So filled with Your Spirit and shaped by Your Hand

That all others see is Thee.

Amen.

In the Words of Wigglesworth...

"We must know that the baptism of the Spirit immerses us into an intensity of zeal, into a likeness to Jesus, to make us into pure, running metal, so hot for God that it travels like oil from vessel to vessel."

Ye Are Our Epistle (Part One), p. 4.

"That the trial of your faith, being much more precious than gold that perisheth, though it be tried with fire, might be found unto praise and honor and glory at the appearing of Christ Jesus." — 1 Peter 1:7

Baptize Me, Holy Spirit

Plunge me, Holy Spirit, into Your ever-flowing stream.
Wash me, Holy Spirit, with His precious blood.
Baptize me, Holy Spirit, with such intense zeal that all I
cherish is Jesus.

> Oh, that I might see Jesus in the mirror of my actions.
> Oh, that I might hear Jesus in the echo of my words.
> Oh, that I might feel Jesus flowing in my veins.

Purify me in His likeness.
> Melt me in His fire.
>> Pour me out a fiery, molten oil to anoint all life
>> around me with Your power and grace. Amen.

Topical Index

Topical Index

Bibliography

The materials quoted in this book are preserved in the archives of the Assemblies of God in Springfield, Missouri. We would like to thank the staff of the archives and their director, Dr. Wayne Warren, for their gracious assistance in our research of the following sermons, notes, Bible studies, letters and pamphlets of Smith Wigglesworth.

"The Abiding Spirit," address presented in Adelaide, Australia, n.d.

"Believe! The Way to Overcome," Faith Leaflet No. 1, n.d.

"Christ in Us," pamphlet (North Melbourne, Australia: Victory Press, n.d.).

"The Cry of the Spirit," n.p., August 1925.

"Divine Life Brings Divine Health," pamphlet (North Melbourne, Australia: Victory Press, n.d.).

"Extraordinary," Faith Booklet No. 2, n.d.

"Faith," Faith Booklet No. 1, n.d.

"Faith (Part One)," message presented at Glad Tidings Tabernacle, 2 August 1922.

"Faith (Part Two)," message presented at Glad Tidings Tabernacle, 3 August 1922.

"Filled With God," address presented in Melbourne, Australia, n.d.

"Floodtide," Faith Leaflet No. 2, n.d.

"Gifts of Healing," Bible study no. 16, n.d.

"The Glory of the Incorruptible," Bible study no. 13, 26 July 1927.

"God Bless You!," Bible study no. 4, 8 July 1927.

"The Incarnation of Man," (North Melbourne, Australia: Victory Press, n.d.) reprinted from the pamphlet "Good News."

"Is Anyone Sick?" n.p., n.d.

"Now! Now! Now!," address presented in Colombier, Switzerland, n.d.

"Ordination," address presented in Adelaide, Australia, n.d.

"Our Calling (Part One)," message presented at Glad Tidings Tabernacle, 18 August 1922.

"Our Calling (Part Two)," message presented at Glad Tidings Tabernacle, 22 August 1922.

"Possession of the Rest," address presented in Wellington, New Zealand, 14 January 1924.

"Rising Into the Heavenlies," address presented in Wellington, New Zealand, 24 January 1924.

"Sons of God," Bible study no. 7, 14 July 1927.

A teaching on 2 Corinthians 3, Bible study no. 16, 29 July 1927.

A teaching on Ephesians 4:1-16, Bible study no. 9, 19 July 1927.

A teaching on John 7:37-39, n.p., n.d.

"Temptation Endured," Bible study no. 12, 22 July 1927.

"That I May Know Him," message presented at Glad Tidings Tabernacle, 20 August 1922.

"Unconditional Surrender" n.p., n.d.

"Workers Together With God," Bible study no. 15, 28 July 1927.

"Ye Are Our Epistle (Part One)," message presented at Glad Tidings Tabernacle, 23 August 1922.

If you enjoyed *Praying With Smith Wigglesworth,* we would like to recommend:

The Smith Wigglesworth Devotional Series

This is the first work of Smith Wigglesworth published in a daily devotional format. Using the original words of Smith Wigglesworth, edited in simple, easy-to-grasp nuggets, each devotion will inspire, motivate and shed insight on God and His faithfulness. Day by day you will be intrigued to find fresh material on faith, healing and prayer that hasn't been available since the 1920s.

Available at your local Christian bookstore or from:

Creation House
600 Rinehart Road
Lake Mary, FL 32746
1-800-283-8494
Web site: http://www.strang.com